GREAT WESTERN COACHES IN COLOUR

Compiled by Kevin Robertson

© Noodle Books (Kevin Robertson) 2011

ISBN 978-1-906419-62-2

First published in 2011 by Kevin Robertson under the **NOODLE BOOKS** imprint
PO Box 279, Corhampton, SOUTHAMPTON. SO32 3ZX

The Publisher and Author hereby give notice that all rights to this work are reserved.
Aside from brief passages for the purpose of review, no part of this work may be reproduced, copied by electronic or other means, or otherwise stored in any information storage and retrieval system without written permission from the Publisher. This includes the illustrations herein which shall remain the copyright of the copyright holder unless otherwise stated.

---

www.noodlebooks.co.uk

Printed in England by Ian Allan Printing.

Front cover - On the coast at Towyn in June / July 1956. Collett 2251 class 0-6-0 No. 2207 awaits departure along the Cambrian Coast line towards Barmouth and beyond with at least three 1920s vintage vehicles. Leading is a 57' steel-panelled Diagram E115, corridor-composite, built to Lot. No. 1324 in 1923 with running numbers in the 76xx series. Next comes a four-compartment Brake-Third to Diagram D95 of 1927/8 and finally, what appears to be part of a Diagram C54 56' bow-ended eight-compartment third of 1926.
Paul Hersey collection

Rear cover - A 54xx 0-6-0PT on the Denham - Uxbridge auto working, circa 1947. The trailer is of Type / Diagram 'L' (both words have been used in previous literature although the GWR used 'Diagram') and of 70' length. Notice the cast letter 'B' carried on the engine: different letters were carried at the front and rear of services on the Greenford branch and signified the operating schedule of that particular service.
John Chamney

Preceding page - Former Restaurant Car No. 9527 recorded as departmental No. 079128 (both the 'W' prefix and suffix are superfluous) outside Swindon shed, 10 July 1963. This vehicle had been completed on 23 June 1906, one of pair of Concertina type First Diners to Diagram H14, Lot No. 1115. At the time, these massive 70' x 9' vehicles - hence the recessed doors, were carried on 4-wheel bogies and took the running numbers 405/6, shortly afterwards changed to 8405/6 and then post 1907, to 9526/7. (The 'W' letter came after 1948.) The car was rebuilt and modernised around January 1939 at which time it also acquired the 6-wheel bogies seen here. It was still in use operating between Swindon and Gloucester circa 1960 but found its last use seemingly as office accommodation, from outside at least it seems to have retained some of its interior fittings including table lamps.
Roy Denison

Opposite - The strap may not have the initials but the securing stud certainly does. Recorded, of all places, inside a coach on the Talyllyn Railway.
Amyas Crump

INTRODUCTION

There is one advantage to being a publisher and that is the opportunity, on occasions, to pursue a whim. To be fair that whim must (in these days of harsh economic reality) have some modicum or chance for success, but I will make no excuses, the compilation of this particular volume has for many years been in my mind - mostly as little more than a whim.

I will also freely admit that I have also had a leaning to one type of Great Western coach, not as might perhaps be expected the Super Saloons or Centenary stock (both of these are represented in the following pages), but instead the more ordinary main-line vehicles and to be even more precise, the Hawksworth designs. Indeed it is for this reason that the illustrations commence on page 6 with this particular design. I suspect this leaning comes from the fact that these were the first Great Western (should I really say Western Region as many of these vehicles were built post 1948?), well Great Western design vehicles in which I recall travelling. Their lush interior (to me at least) creating a particular impression, heavily sprung seats, polished woodwork and armrests which could be raised or lowered from the back, far superior to the Southern Region DEMUs which were the only other regular vehicles in which I travelled at the time. (Later I came to appreciate the Bulleid designs and BR Mk1s, but that is indeed another story.) Consequently everything about a Hawksworth was, to a child of tender years, impressive. How could there be any comparison with the Formica and aluminium of the modern diesel?

Later I would read that to many the exterior design of the Hawksworth was clumsy - so what. More poignantly they were destined to have a very short life in the top flight of Western Region service, hence the cascade policy on to the secondary route where I had become acquainted with them. (More on this topic in the captions.)

But away from the nostalgia and to return to fact. Having been privileged to publish Michael Welch's book on 'Southern Coaches in Colour' (Noodle Books - 2010), it occurred this might just be the time to resurrect my own idea from the past. Despite being fortunate to have ascribed a wide range of contacts over the years whom I might approach for images, it quickly became apparent that this would be no easy quest. It was also not helped by my own self imposed criteria: 'No views of trains where the excuse would be to say, "The eighth vehicle back (totally indistinguishable of course) is a …...type…(whatever)", and also no preservation.'. Both were to prove an impossible task and consequently I have had to relinquish these ideals on the basis of pure reality. Even so there are some absolute gems that have come to light and for this I must thank all those mentioned overleaf, without their help to what at times must have appeared to be a seeming constant stream of e-mails and telephone calls, this book would have been definitely the poorer.

Even so there are still considerable gaps. Understandably people photographed trains. Colour images of solo coaches are as rare as the proverbial. Indeed whilst there is a veritable plethora of 'train' shots it is a fingers of one hand (with a few gaps as well) when attempting to find individual coach views. Hence the need for limited compromise - as referred to earlier.

Despite also my comments about having a favourite, I have tried to include images of what I know are others' favourites as well. Consequently you will find examples of the Super Saloons, other Special Saloons, and of course the two Dynamometer cars. (One of these was a converted Hawksworth design 'Third'.)

At the other end of the scale we have the ubiquitous auto-trailer, camping coaches, the odd toplight (wonderful!) a few engineers vehicles, some Collett stock, a clerestory or two and ……...well one or two absolutely wonderful scenes: I am sure all would agree that the very first page comes into this latter category.

Considering also my comments about the ideals versus the practicalities, I have taken the opportunity to include a few views of vehicles in their correct context, in trains, but please recall, this has been done on as few occasions as possible and not as a substitute for the reasons stated earlier.

Turning the pages that follow may, hopefully, recall a few memories. Fortunately there were those, a generation or more ago, who recognised the need for rolling stock, in this case coaches, to be preserved as well as locomotives. I salute then the preservationists of the Great Western Society, Severn Valley Railway, and West Somerset Railway in particular.

Whilst we may now regret the passing of certain coach types, it might also be appropriate to recall the ones that got away and not just in the tangible sense. When I started this quest I recall speaking to a friend of many years standing, Rob Thompson, and naturally asked him if he had any relevant material.

Rob's reply was to recall the line of old coaches, 'Dreadnoughts' included, which had for some time stood alongside the main line at Old Oak Common in the sixties. Rob mentioned he had taken several colour images of these - but quickly tempered my enthusiasm with the words, "The processor ruined the film, there was nothing…....by the time I discovered this and went back they had of course all gone".

Fortunately the ones you will see on the following pages were the ones that did not get away, on film at least.

Kevin Robertson

ACKNOWLEDGMENTS AND BIBLIOGRAPHY

It is with grateful thanks that I acknowledge the assistance of the various photographers and friends whose work or assistance has been invaluable to this project:

Austin Attewell
Pat Avery
David Barker
Julian Bowden
Graham Carpenter
John Chamney
Paul Chancellor (Colour Rail)
Amyas Crump
Brian Dale
Roy Denison
Peter Elliott
Antony Ford
Jim Gander
Alan Garner
Brian J Harding
Mike Hudson
Steve Jordan
Phil Kelley
John Lewis
Rodney Lissenden
(- as custodian to the collection of the late R C Riley).
Roy Mears
Mike Morant
Bruce Murray
Barry Mursell
David Smith
Rob Thompson
Adrian Vaughan
Peter Waller
Lawrence Waters - for access to the Great Western Society archive.

Also to Graham Carpenter, Amyas Crump, David Hyde and John Palk, all of whom were 'persuaded' to read the draft!

Preserved GWR Coaches listed on the internet: http://www.uksteam.info/gwr/hs.htm

The following published works have been consulted:

Great Western Coaches from 1890 - Michael Harris (3rd Edition)
David & Charles 1984
A Pictorial Record of Great Western Coaches. Part 1: 1838-1913 - J H Russell
Oxford Publishing Co.
A Pictorial Record of Great Western Coaches. Part 2: 1903-1948 - J H Russell
Oxford Publishing Co.
Great Western Coaches Appendix. Vol. 1 and 2 - J H Russell
Oxford Publishing Co.
Great Western Auto-Trailers, Parts 1 & 2 - John Lewis
Wild Swan Publications
Scenes From the Past : Part 2 British Railways Camping Coach Holidays -
Andrew McRae   Foxline Publishing
Camp Coach Holidays on the GWR - Mike Fenton
Wild Swan Publications
The Kingsbridge Branch - Ken Williams   Oxford Publishing Co.
Preserved Railway Carriages - John Lloyd   Silver Link Publishing
The Western Dynamometer Car - T D Allen Civil
Odd Corners of the GWR - Kevin Robertson
Alan Sutton / Reprinted by The History Press
GW & WR Restaurant Cars 2nd Edition. - Colin Strevens, Edited by M J Cornick
Monmouthshire Railway Society
Railway News Stockbook of ex GWR and BR (WR) Push/Pull Auto Coaches 5th Edition.   Railway Publishing Society

CONTENTS

The Hawksworth Era (Main Line Stock)	7
Mr. Collett's Trains	15
The super 'Super-Saloons'	16
Parcels stock	28
Collett stock in service	31
'Toplights' and Camping Coaches	32
Specialist Vehicles: The Churchward Dynamometer Car and the Whitewash Coach	41
Restaurant Cars	44
Special Saloons and Inspection Saloons	50
The Auto-Trailer Breed	57
Relics from an Earlier Age	62

A veritable feast of 'Great Westernery' at Tiverton Junction - apart that is from the liveries. The 'Hall' is waiting for its own signal before departing north towards Taunton, the steam from the safety valve obscuring the single line to Hemyock on the right. To the left is a glimpse of a 14xx: taking water whilst working the Tiverton branch service.

The roof detail and side is from a Hawksworth Brake Corridor Third of the type built between 1947 and 1953 and seen from the compartment side.

Left - Because of their short time in front line service before being ousted by the BR Mk1 type from 1951 onwards, views of complete trains of Hawksworth stock on prestige workings are rare - indeed none has yet been located showing a complete rake of this stock in chocolate and cream. A full rake in 'blood and custard' is equally unusual, hence the inclusion of the top left image of No. 6013 'King Henry VIII' and Hawksworth train recorded in 1953. To be fair the profile alone indicates that further back the restaurant portion is of at least Collett vintage: no public catering vehicles built to the Hawksworth design. The location is Lavington on the Berks and Hants route. *Colour Rail BRW1346 / P M Alexander*

At **lower left** the location is clearly the Bristol line from Reading. No 7308 is in charge of the 12.18 Hastings to Birmingham, a mixed rake, consisting of a Hawksworth, followed by a Mk1, and at least two more Hawksworths'. 1954.   *Colour Rail BRW808*

Bottom right, how the mighty have fallen. Hawksworth stock already pensioned off on to cross-country and branch line duty when probably little more than 10 years old. The location is Highclere on the DNS line sometime between 1957 and March 1960.   *David Smith.*

THE HAWKSWORTH ERA (MAIN LINE STOCK)

The Hawksworth design for main line coaches is admirably summed up by the late Michael Harris as 'Post-War Hopes Frustrated'. Had the opportunity presented itself then the vehicles would have incorporated fluorescent lighting, 'Empire veneers' for panelling, laminated plastic panelling ('Formica') and specially woven materials for the internal furnishing. In the event these innovations were only ever seen on the prototype. Shortages of materials prevented much of this innovation, although 'Third' No. 784 was fitted out with 'Formica' in 1948, the colours chosen: a combination of duck egg blue and iron grey: a mixture the travelling public would become very familiar with in later years! At 64' in length, the new design was four feet longer than pre-war designs (excluding of course the 70' vehicles of the Churchward era), the additional space in the new vehicles allowing for larger compartments and bigger vestibules. Despite this increase in size, there was a welcome lessening in weight, pre-war equivalent main-line stock tipping the scales at between 31½-34 tons, whilst the new build was between 30-32 tons. (Brake vehicles were the lightest and first class the heaviest. These figures do not include the Hawksworth sleeping cars.) Again a prototype with an aluminium underframe was produced, but this was not repeated for the production vehicles.

A 1967 view of Hawksworth 'Third' W890W to Diagram C82 - the location is not stated. This was one of the first batch of vehicles to this particular design produced and built for the GWR by the Gloucester Carriage & Wagon Company. A total of 152 identical 'Thirds' would eventually be built. The principal aesthetic features were the flat (slab) sides instead of the more conventional tumblehome, also bow ends to the roof. The decision to provide four access doors on either side led to the mix of window sizes on the corridor side and consequent accusation of an untidy appearance. On the opposite side it also resulted in two of the compartments having their own access doors. Whilst the additional openings may have been fine in theory, in practice the compartments so affected were the least popular: passengers finding discomfort as others brushed past with bags and luggage. Eight compartments were provided and there was also a lavatory at each end. Withdrawal of the Hawksworth corridor stock commenced in early 1965, although three vehicles, all former 'Thirds' now designated 'Corridor-Seconds', W1719W, W2135W and W2283W, received BR 'Blue-Grey' at Wolverton (Swindon had ceased carriage overhaul in 1965). In their new livery they were used between Plymouth and Penzance on London trains which had a trolley refreshment service: believed to be as the trolley would fit into a Hawksworth compartment as a base from which to operate from - the trolley being too wide to fit into a Mk1 compartment. (All three in their corporate blue/grey identity were also seen on one occasion at Kings Cross.) It was to be a short lived venture into the 'modern' age, as all passenger carrying Hawksworth stock was withdrawn from public service at the end of 1967. (A photograph of a train incorporating a blue/grey vehicle in this form appears at http://freepages.nostalgia.rootsweb.com/~cyberheritage/oldy2.jpg .) *Colour Rail 81076*

HAWKSWORTH MAIN LINE STOCK

LOT	LOT COMPLETED (*Total Built*)	TYPE	DIA. No.	DIMENSIONS Ft. Ins Ft. Ins	RUNNING NOS.	NOTES	PRESERVED
1685	29/4/1950? *1*	Third	C.85	64. 0 8. 11	2239	Experimental	
1688	19/11/49 *4*	First	A.23	64. 0 8. 11	8001-3		
1689	23/10/48 *11*	Composite	E.163	64. 0 8. 11	7252-62		
1690	25/12/48 *14*	Brake Composite	E.164	64. 0 8. 11	7372-85	Nos. 7372 & 7377 used for Royal Train service. 7374-76 converted for slip coach working 1958	7372, 7377
1691	12/6/48 *52*	Third	C.82	64. 0 8. 11	781-832	No. 796 converted to Dynamometer Car in 1961	825
1692	27/12/47 *22*	Brake Third	D.131	64. 0 8. 11	833-54		
1702	17/2/51 *4*	First Sleeper	J.18	64. 0 9. 1¾	9082-5	12-wheel	
1703	28/1/50 *12*	First	A.23	64. 0 8. 11	8053-64		
1704	5/11/49 *19*	Composite	E.165	64. 0 8. 11	7798-7816	7817-22 cancelled	
1705	30/7/48 *10*	Brake Composite	E.164	64. 0 8. 11	7838-47	7848-67 cancelled. See Lot 1738	
1706	16/4/49 *25*	Third	C.84	64. 0 8. 11	1713-37	1738-62 cancelled	
1707	2/7/49 *15*	Brake Third	D.133	64. 0 8. 11	1772-86	Built B'ham RCW 1787-96 cancelled	
1708		*Third*		64. 0 8. 11	*1797-1806*	*Lots cancelled*	
1709		*Brake Third*		64. 0 8. 11	*1807-10*	*Ordered 24/5/46*	
1710		*Composite*		64. 0 8. 11	*7416-25*		
1711		*Brake Composite*		64. 0 8. 11	*7386-7405*		
1714	27/11/48 *70*	Third	C.82	64. 0 8. 11	855-924	Built Gloucester RCW	
1720	30/4/49 *30*	Third	C.82	64. 0 8. 11	2107-36	Built Gloucester RCW	
1722	3/12/49 *100*	Passenger Brake	K.45	64. 0 8. 11	290-99	Similar order cancelled	295,297
1732	4/11/50 *100*	Brake Third	D.133	64. 0 8. 11	2137-85 / 2187-2223 / 2225-38	Last Lot ordered by GWR. Built B'ham RCW	2202,2214,2216,2218, 2225,2232,2233
1734	1/7/50 *14*	First	A.23	64. 0 8. 11	8112-25		
1735	22/4/50 *29*	Third	C.84	64. 0 8. 11	2264-92		
1737	9/9/50 *6*	Composite	E.165	64. 0 8. 11	7817-22		
1738	30/12/50 *20*	Brake Composite	E.164	64. 0 8. 11	7848-67		
1740	25/11/50 *25*	Passenger Brake	K.45	64. 0 8. 11	300-24		316
1744	20/1/51 *20*	Brake Third	D.133	64. 0 8. 11	2240-59	Built Metro-Cammell	
1752	7/7/51 *10*	Passenger Brake	K.46	64. 0 8. 11	325-34		333,334

The corridor side of W2264W in 1967, a corridor third to Diagram C84. This order, Lot No. 1732, was for 29 identical vehicles and was placed by the Western Region. (Notwithstanding the post 1948 built date, a number of Hawksworth vehicles were still delivered in chocolate and cream livery, although possibly this applied more to those constructed by outside contractors.) The same unsymmetrical window spacing applied on this, the compartment side, necessitated by the access doors at two of the compartments. Two of the advantages of the 64' length, the additional compartment width and larger vestibules have already been mentioned, both features assisted by having access doors within the compartments so saving the space for a right-angle corridor in the centre of the coach leading to a single door. The large windows came in for some criticism, one passenger comparing these with similar fittings on the LNER and 'want to cause sickness due to the speed of passage'. Clearly said passenger had never travelled in the earlier 'centenary' stock! The positioning of the brackets for roofboards was on the cantrail: previous GWR designs had the boards placed above the cantrail. Maroon did not quite suit these vehicles, a two-tone colour scheme was definitely to their advantage. The battery boxes were also directly opposite each other.   *Colour Rail 81041*

These pages show the two sides of a Brake Third vehicle both to Diagram D133. ***Above*** *is No. W2253W built by the Birmingham Railway Carriage & Wagon Co. and recorded in 1967.* ***Opposite*** *is W1777W from Metropolitan Cammell. Three batches of this type were built, the design consisting of four third-class passenger compartments, that nearest the Guard / Luggage space having an access door on each side. On the compartment side there was also an additional single passenger door between this last compartment and the door for the Guard. This extra door justifiably gave rise to the comment as to its necessity. The three large compartment windows each had a sliding ventilator (the fourth compartment referred to had a droplight to the door). Notice that on the corridor side there was a single sliding ventilator to just one window. Also, the brackets for the 'roof' boards at cantrail level: these were central to the passenger accommodation rather than in the middle of the coach itself. A single toilet was provided. Whilst comment has already been made reference the window spacing of the Hawksworth vehicles, it should not be forgotten that this mix of picture window and ventilator fitted window had been seen pre-war on the circa 1938 Collett stock. In these however, there was a degree of uniformity as well as symmetry surrounding the design - see illustration of a Diagram C77 Corridor Third in maroon to the left of the former slip coach. On Page 11, No. W1777W, right, has clearly been put to grass and with its tell-tale 'hot-cross bun' symbol has carried its last passengers, the date would therefore be sometime between 1965 and 1967. The locations of the views are not stated. Several vehicles of this Diagram type have been preserved.*

Above: Colour Rail 81092 - Opposite: Amyas Crump - ***Opposite inset -*** *Moquette design from a Hawksworth Brake Third. John Palk.*

10

A wonderful example of a Diagram E164, Brake Composite built in 1948, No. W7377W, comprising four third class compartments of 6' 2" width and two first class compartments of 7' 3" width, the latter nearest the guard's accommodation. A swing door (hinged at the window side) separated the classes, each was also provided with an individual lavatory. Naturally to accommodate this passenger accommodation, the available space in the guard / luggage compartment was severely curtailed, indeed the latter was to a maximum 9' 8" only. A total of 44 of the type seen were built in three separate Lots: it would have been more had others not been cancelled - see table on page 8. Along with No. 7372 of the same Diagram, both these vehicles were allocated new to Old Oak Common and used almost exclusively on special workings. They were also formed as part of the Western Region Royal Train (together with saloons Nos. 9006/7). No doubt at the behest of Paddington, the two also sported GWR livery until 1957 when they migrated to the standard WR chocolate and cream livery seen. This particular example was acquired by the Dart Valley Railway (now the South Devon Railway) and is depicted in the condition as it arrived at Buckfastleigh. Sister vehicle No. 7372 is preserved by the Great Western Society at Didcot.
Amyas Crump

Main view - *In 1958 three Hawksworth Brake-Composite vehicles to the same diagram (E164) and Lot as that seen left, were converted to double ended slip coaches with the corridor connections removed, the requisite observation windows added and fitted with additional vacuum cylinders. These were Nos. 7374-6 which retained their original numbers. By this time only three trains had slip portions, the Weymouth slip off the down 'Cornish Riviera' - slipped at Heywood Road outside Westbury, the up 7.00 am Weston-Super-Mare to Paddington which slipped at Didcot, and the 5.10 pm Paddington - Wolverhampton which slipped at Bicester. All three vehicles were painted in WR chocolate and cream although at least one (and probably the others), No. W7376W had appeared in standard maroon by 1963. Slip coach working ended with the Bicester slip on 9 September 1960 after which all three had their slip couplings replaced with standard draw-gear and were transferred to Taunton in early 1961 for use on the secondary / branch lines to Barnstaple, Minehead, and Chard as well as on main-line stopping services. (there is a b/w illustration of No. W7376W at Oxford in 1963 in the Michael Harris book). In the illustration above, taken at Barnstaple Junction, and after a return to conventional duty, the additional vacuum cylinders will be noted. At left is an example of a Corridor Third, having eight compartments and built to Diagram. C77 around 1938*

Brian J Harding

Inset - *An unidentified member of the trio out of use at Highbridge but included to show the positioning of the end windows.*

Amyas Crump

In 1961, a former Corridor Third, No. 796 to Diagram C82, Lot No. 1691 of 1946, was taken out of public service, stripped internally, and converted for use as a new Dynamometer Car for the Western Region. Certain of the technical equipment from the 1901 Churchward Dynamometer Car being re-fitted into the new vehicle. In keeping with tradition, the coach was turned out in full chocolate and cream - complete with GWR coat of arms prominently displayed in the conference room. Although at this time BR and consequently WR technical trials were almost exclusively restricted to the testing of new diesel locomotives, main line testing on the line between Oxford and Worcester did take place with an 'Austerity' 0-6-0T fitted with a mechanical-stoker. (An illustration of a conventional C82 seen from the corridor side appears on page 7.) Upon conversion, the vehicle was given the number DW150192, but subsequently carried 'Test car No. 4' and then No. 99140. As regional autonomy waned so the vehicle was transferred to the Railway Technical Centre at Derby in 1967, but remained in use until 1983. It has since been preserved. (See also page 42/43 reference the earlier Dynamometer Car.)

Top left - At Oxford shed on 28 March 1963, probably in connection with the steam trial referred to. The unique WR upper quadrant signals may just be discerned in the left background. *Julian Bowden collection*

Bottom left - At Laira, 30 August 1961. (Trials with steam had also taken place even at this late stage: on 11 July 1961 with No. 5056 'Earl of Powis' for 'moderate speed' testing on clipping up and down of AWS and then on 16 and 27 July 1961 using the same engine for higher speed tests.)   *R C Riley*

Above - An example of a 'passenger brake' to Hawksworth design, No. W321 to Diagram K45 recorded at Reading in the 1970s. As can be seen, non passenger carrying stock tended to have a longer spell of useful life, as witness the blue livery. Several examples of this and the similar K46 diagram vehicles have entered preservation.   *Barry Mursell*

Mr COLLETT'S TRAINS

(Great) Western finery at Brecon. Collett 2251 class 0-6-0 No. 2218 on a three coach local, the first vehicle of which is an example of a 57' flat ended 'high waist' Brake Composite of 1933, Lot No. 1491 to Diagram E146. Just ten of these vehicles were built in the series 6579-88, with four Third-Class, two First-Class compartments, a single lavatory and Guard / Luggage accommodation. Although not visible from the illustration, it is interesting to note that both battery boxes on these coaches were located underneath the corridor side. In the bay is clearly another Hawksworth, behind which No. W6620W, a Diagram E151 Flat-Ended Composite, 58' 7" in length dating from 1936. Again just ten of these particular vehicles were built, the number scheme not following in sequence and instead covering Nos. 6606/7/11/2/4/7/8/20/2/3. This particular Diagram were known as 'Sunshine' stock. Both the vehicles described in detail were carried on 9' bogies. No vehicles from either Diagram survived into preservation.
Colour Rail BRW239

THE SUPER 'SUPER SALOONS'

The eight 'Super Saloons' built by the GWR in 1931 rank amongst the best known and most easily identified of all the Swindon built vehicles. The type had its origins in the 1929 'Riviera' stock, whilst the later 1935 'Centenary' coaches again displayed a family likeness. Their purpose was a simple desire by the GWR to afford a luxury service at a cheaper rate than had been achieved with the hire of Pullman vehicles and attendants, as tried out on the 'Torquay Pullman' during 1929. In addition Pullman coaches had been included in the formation of some of Plymouth boat trains. With their arrival in service, the new saloons took over the prestige workings and although officially known as 'Super Saloons' the names 'Pullman', 'Cunard' or 'Ocean Saloon' stock was used. The vehicles were also much used for private-hire and on the Member's Newbury Race trains. Although rarely reported as running as a rake of eight vehicles plus brake(s) (no brake-end super-saloons were constructed), it was not unknown for one or more to be included in the formation of a 'Royal', especially when this was included as part of an ordinary service train. Their use on Plymouth workings continued until as late as the end of 1962, after which BR were no longer able to deal with liners at Plymouth. They were then to be seen employed for party travel, as well as continuing on the Newbury workings referred to.

Left - Possibly running for a special party, W9117W, the former 'Princess Mary', is seen at Snow Hill. Under the GWR, all eight vehicles had been named, although these ceased to be carried sometime after 1948. Post 1948 under BR, the livery was changed to standard 'crimson and cream' although all were repainted in WR chocolate and cream from 1957. *Amyas Crump*

Top right - A Plymouth boat train arriving at Paddington. Michael Harris reports that in 1956 a typical train of this type might comprise: a bogie brake, Hawksworth brake-composite, two second-corridors, restaurant-second No. 9626, 'Super Saloon' No. 9115, Kitchen car No. 9663, 'Super Saloons' Nos. 9113/2 and a further bogie-brake. In the view seen, that nearest the camera is No. W9115W, the former 'Duke of Gloucester'. *Amyas Crump*

Bottom right: W9117W as part of a Royal formation at Paddington. (No 9004/5 is to the right.) *Jim Gander*

Inset - A 'Trollope' lamp from No. 9117. *Amyas Crump*

17

Top left - *When not in use, the Super Saloons were stabled at the bottom end of the carriage shed at Old Oak Common under the eye of the carriage inspector. They were also kept clean ready for immediate use. Here, Nos. 9117 and 9118 await their next duty. All afforded First Class only accommodation.*   *Amyas Crump*

Bottom left *- Special duty for No. 9117, part of the make up of a service train recorded passing Pershore. (The saloon was the second vehicle in the train hauled by a spotless 'Castle'.) Both No. 9117 and 9118 had been rebuilt by the GWR in 1935 to incorporate a small kitchen: hence the double access doors. This enabled them to be used as independent VIP vehicles. Compare the side profile of this vehicle having a kitchen with those seen top-right on page 17. Originally built to Lot 1471, Diagram No. G60 applied to Nos. 9111/2, and G61 to the remainder. This was due to a variation in interior furnishing - see interior caption on next page.*   *Brian J Harding*

Above *- Just out of service and with an interim undercoat applied prior to full restoration. This is No. 9111, the former 'King George' seen at Totnes and now preserved at Buckfastleigh. No. 9111 was the only one of its type that had carried maroon under BR. Of the eight vehicles, two, Nos 9115 and 9117, were taken out of service in October 1965. Five, Nos. 9111, 9112, 9113, 9116 and 9118 were purchased for preservation.*   *John Palk*

Above - No. 9111, the former 'King George' along with a BG brake and No. 9113 at Bodmin Road on 26 July 1962. The vehicles were part of the train being used for the Royal Tour of the Duchy of Cornwall. On this date a cold buffet was being served to members of the tour support staff. On the left is Ted Hocking in his Chauffeur's uniform, to the right is Mr Robins; Head of New Works at Plymouth, who had been responsible for ensuring the Super Saloons could travel in Cornwall.

Left - Believed to be W9117W (otherwise it will be No. 9118) being shunted at Paddington in 1964.

Both - John Chamney

Left - As will be gathered from the exterior illustrations, the Super Saloons were built to take advantage of the maximum, 9' 7" width available from the GWR loading gauge, whilst ideal for normal service it did restrict their use, all then being branded 'Red Triangle'. The interiors were furnished to a high standard, the first two by Messrs. Trollope & Sons and the remainder a combination of this firm and Swindon. Seating was flexible, allowing for a '1+1' arrangement instead of the '2+1' seen here. At the time of their introduction, passengers were required to pay a 10/- supplement to the normal First Class fare - this was higher than both the contemporary Pullman supplement charged elsewhere and greater also than the levy for the LNER 'Silver Jubilee' service. Post-war, all eight vehicles were renovated and refurbished, this work included new windows having deeper ventilators as well as the obvious replacement carpets and upholstery.

Roy Denison

Right - In sparkling livery, W9115W, the former 'Duke of Gloucester' at Plymouth Millbay - Chief Inspector Pollard in attendance alongside. The roofboard proclaims 'Pacific Line via Plymouth'.

John Chamney

To commemorate the centenary of the GWR in 1935, Swindon introduced the appropriately named 'Centenary' stock. Similar in outline style to the Super Saloons, here was a range of new stock intended for the prestige workings of the GWR although compared with the Saloons, these new vehicles were intended for general use, hence conventional compartments were provided. The design consisted 'Brake Third' - 6 vehicles built; D120: 'Corridor Third' - 6 vehicles built, C69. 'Corridor Composite' - 4 vehicles built; E149: Brake Composite' 6 vehicles built; E150: 'First Class Diner (Restaurant)', H43, and 'Third Class Dining Saloon', H44; 2 of each built, both the latter formed as pairs. Seen above is Brake Third No. W4576W at Birmingham Snow Hill. This was one of four vehicles from the batch (the others were Nos. 4575/8/9) which were right handed, Nos 4577 / 80 being left handed. Both were to the same Lot No. 1536, and identical Diagram No. D120. As built, all had drop-style windows fitted to both the compartment and corridor sides but these were subsequently changed between 1936-38 to windows with conventional sliding vents, as seen here. For much of the time the vehicles ran in sets, and according to Michael Harris, were considered superior to other 'Big-Four' corridor coaches. Post war only one full set was in regular use, between Weston-super-Mare and Paddington. Otherwise the dining pairs continued working between Paddington and Shrewsbury. Again quoting Michael Harris, "...like the pre-war élite of the LMS and LNER, they ended their days in relief and slow trains. Centenary Restaurant No. 9636 has the distinction of being the final GWR design Restaurant Car on a regular daily working out of Paddington and continued this until the autumn of 1962. Restaurant No 9635 has been preserved at Didcot as the sole example of this design of stock to have survived. Otherwise all stock to the 'Centenary' design was withdrawn from 1962 onwards and rendered extinct in 1964. (See also page 47.)   *Amyas Crump*

Rural Devon at its best - believed to be the Tavistock branch. (The temptation is to say the view is on the Princetown branch but David Smith was not taking images when this was operational.) The single coach is an example of a Collett Brake-Third, 4-compartment Bow-ended 'General Service Stock'. Two Lots of this design, Nos. 1476 and 1478, Diagram D115 were produced, both completed in 1932 and totalling 22 vehicles. In appearance they were very similar to the Diagram D105, stock for the 'Cornish Riviera' built in 1929, the one visual difference being the latter did not have roof ventilators over the luggage compartment. Again both left and right hand corridor examples were provided. The eight vehicles built to Lot 1476 were originally intended to form four five-car sets coupled to a composite and third, with vehicles from Lots 1474 and 1475, respectively Diagram E.144 and C.62 stock. Most of the carriages of this type were withdrawn in 1962.

David Smith

Brake Third Corridor coach, No. W4118W in the winter sun at Stratford-upon-Avon, 14 December 1957. This was a 1936 built vehicle, one of 66 to Lot 1555, Diagram D121, the number series being 4066-69, 4073-4102, and 4104-25. (As with other designs, the reason for the gaps in the running numbers is not immediately obvious, could it perhaps refer to left or right corridor examples, although to be fair all the images seen of D121 vehicles show a corridor on the same side.*) Diagram D121 were four-compartment vehicles, with, it will be noted, droplights that sit slightly higher than the level of the larger windows. Built to dimensions of 60' 11¼" x 9' 0", there was a similar design All-Third to Diagram C70 constructed at the same time. Shortly afterwards a second batch of the C70 type were built, again in 1936. The total of C70 vehicles being 68 coaches. According to Russell, vehicles to Diagram D121 were condemned in December 1963. None, of either D121 or C70 survived into preservation.   *R C Riley*

* Graham Carpenter makes the following suggestion, "If the GWR had wanted to differentiate between left / right corridor vehicles they could have used another Diagram No. for the same Lot, as was done elsewhere. Although on things GW, there was always an exception! When GWR vehicles were scrapped, numbers could be reused. For new builds a block of numbers would be issued but sometimes odd random numbers were used up - particularly some wagon Lots could have nearly all odd numbers, i.e. not in a block. So perhaps the gaps are due to existing, say Welsh Railway numbered coaches?"

This page, top - A 'King' hauled express at Hatton (well that was the easy bit!) Under the glass the number of this vehicle appears to be similar to 4625, however clearly that cannot be exactly correct as this number was allocated to a 57' brake-third and this is certainly a 70' vehicle. It falls then into either D82, D84 or possibly D90 type, all 70' 0" x 9' 0" brake-third vehicles having four compartments and a considerable space for luggage. The difference between the two diagrams was that on D82 one end was flat the other bowed, whereas with D84 both were flat ends. The image is not distinct enough to confirm. In layout these vehicles, originally built as 'South Wales' stock, were not dissimilar to the final 'Toplight' style of 70' brake vehicles. As new in 1923/24 Diagram D84 vehicles at least, also appeared in a livery sporting pseudo panelling. A total of 20 vehicles were built, being taken out of service probably between 1958 and 1962. None survived.

Amyas Crump

This page, bottom - Llanynynech on the Whitchurch - Aberystwyth line, the carriage board conveniently indicating the eventual destination. From the window spacing the vehicle is probably A Brake-Composite, flat-ended 'General Service' vehicle either to Lot 1508 of 1934 or Lot 1535 of the following year. In both cases Diagram E148 applied. In total 40 were built and measured 57' 0" x 9' 0". All were flat ended and numbered in the 68xx or 69xx series. In BR days they were cascaded into service on secondary and cross country routes and consequently examples could be seen over a wide area. Most were withdrawn towards the end of 1962, coinciding with the closure programme of the various lines over which they had worked. No. 6913 has survived on the Severn Valley Railway.

Mike Hudson

Opposite - Neath Riverside with No 3706 at the head of the 11.25 to Brecon on 28 April 1962, formed of at least two coaches. (The South Wales main line passes over the bridge at the end of the platform.) Nearest the camera and in spanking maroon livery, is W7290W, a Diagram E162 corridor-composite having four first-class and three second-class compartments. Thirty vehicles were built to this Diagram, Lot 1639, in 1941. Numbered 7271-90, they were 59' 10" x 8' 11" and fitted with 9' pressed-steel bogies. Seen is the compartment side, not dissimilar to the Hawksworth outline of just a few years later and again having picture windows of uneven size, none of the corridor windows had sliding ventilators. At the front of the train it is believed is a Brake-Third possibly to Diagram D124, 4-compartment general purpose stock of 1937.

Mike Hudson

SUBURBAN INTERLUDE

Opposite - A wonderful image by the late Dick Riley of the departure of the 17.20 to Severn Beach from Patchway station on 20 September 1955. (Of little consequence perhaps was that 2 6-2T No. 6107 was in charge.) Seventeen years separate the two designs, plus one designer of course. W3955W is a Churchward regime Multibar 8-compartment Toplight Third, to Diagram C35, Lot No. 1256, the last vehicle from this batch was completed on 29 November 1919. This batch of vehicles carried running numbers from 3949 to 3981. The final vehicle is a Collett era Brake Composite of 1936, Diagram E152, Lot No. 1557. Russell points out that contrary to the perceived view of the Great Western being a standardised railway, around the time of construction of this vehicle, coach lengths appeared to vary considerably. Diagram E152 for example being 60' 11¼" x 9' 0", whilst coaches built either side, and to similar visual outline, might be 60' 0" or 58' 7" long, the width however was constant. Numbering was random, the 65 vehicles built carried running numbers either in blocks or singularly between 6859 and 6973. Whilst the external design of the Toplight is clearly of an earlier era, the large picture windows of the Brake Composite still present a relatively modern style, albeit one now approaching 75 years of age.   *R C Riley*

Above - 61xx No. 6151 on a stopping suburban service. Workings such as this were a regular sight of the Great Western and later British Railways scene through to the early 1960s, and in the London area took in both the West of England and Birmingham lines. Non corridor stock features, the first vehicle is a six-compartment Third built by the Gloucester Carriage & Wagon Co. to Diagram D132, Lot No. 1746 in 1952. Vehicles to this diagram had first appeared from Swindon in 1948. A further batch of identical vehicles were constructed by a different outside contractor in 1953. The end windows will be noted. The second vehicle is a BR Standard design suburban coach, the remainder would be subject of speculation only. *Steam & Sail Slides*

Right - Third class seat moquette, circa 1937.   *John Palk*

PARCELS STOCK

Equally as important for revenue, but seemingly rarely recorded by comparison with passenger carrying stock, were the various types of Parcels Vans, most built to and also painted in coaching stock style. (There were also 'Brown Vehicles' so painted post 1922 and more akin to goods stock but fitted with vacuum brakes and other details to allow them to run in passenger trains. Some ordinary goods stock was also fitted and might be used in similar workings - see example on page 22.) The colours were as per the coaching stock of the period, whilst some parcels stock which did survive beyond the 1960s also appeared in the bland BR Blue style - see page 14.

Opposite, top left - W159W, a 12/1937 built Diagram K42, Lot No. 1604, 57' 0" x 8' 11" passenger brake, seen at Thame as the solitary vehicle on the 61xx hauled 6.00 pm parcels to Princess Risborough. The vehicle is branded 'Paddington and Banbury'. 16 May 1964.
Amyas Crump

Opposite, bottom left - This time a K41 of 1934 is recorded, No. W107W is from Lot 1495: the branding seen inset. Although the window spacing was identical with the K42 one dimensional difference, the 9' width, was sufficient to warrant the diagram alteration.   *Amyas Crump*

Opposite, top right – The 10.10 pm Paddington - Penzance Mail / Sleeper service seen in daylight hours at Penzance, 21 June 1957. On the far platform two vehicles may be identified, that immediately behind the locomotive a K40 passenger-brake, believed to be W81W and again branded. The next vehicle is a PO sorting van to Diagram L25.
John Chamney

This page - The 18.40 postal from Penzance seen shortly before departure, 20 June 1957. Behind the 'Hall' is a K38 Passenger Brake of 1934, W1177W, this is followed by a 1947 built PO Sorting Van to Diagram L25, vehicle believed to be No. W846W. The train / vehicles in the near platform is not identified although the milk tanks at the rear will be noted.   *John Chamney*

COLLETT STOCK IN SERVICE

Opposite page - Suburban working at Aylesbury in 1938. Commencing in 1927, large numbers of non-corridor vehicles of three basic types, Brake-Third, Composite, and All-Third, were built. The outline design showing similarity to the successful 'B-Set' concept of 1926. Indeed, suburban vehicles to what was a little altered design continued to be constructed for over 25 years - see caption to image on page 27. A number of suburban vehicles were formed into fixed four-coach rakes consisting a Brake-Thirds at either end and within, a pair of Composites.
Steam and Sail

Above - No. 5954 'Faendre Hall' leaving Box Tunnel towards Corsham in 1956. The four passenger vehicles are all 1930s style stock, leading possibly a Diagram D115 Brake-Third, more certain are the following two vehicles, an E132 Composite followed by a C54 8-compartment Third. The final coach cannot be determined but again could be to Diagram D115.
Colour Rail / P M Alexander BRW1043

TOPLIGHTS AND CAMPING COACHES

The toplight era on the Great Western and its successor, the Western Region lasted over half a century. The first 'Bars 1' vehicles appeared in 1907 with construction continuing at intervals through to 1920. Reference is also made to 'Bars 2' and 'Multibar' vehicles, these describing variations in the underframe as well as changes to the body moulding. (The reader is referred to the Michael Harris coach book for full details of the changes / variation: pages 64 et seq.)

The Toplight design also encompassed both 70' and 57' lengths versions (there were a few variations close to each size) and to a number of carriage types. These were: Brake-Third, Third, First/Third Composite, Tri-Composite, First/Second Composite, Brake-Composite, Single-Slip Composite, Double-Slip Composite, First, Passenger Brake-Van, First Sleeper, and Sleeper Composite. Not surprisingly the shorter length coaches were considerably more numerous. It is interesting to note that not all Toplight vehicles built were provided with corridor connections. A number of coaches to Toplight design were constructed especially for use in Ambulance trains in WW1, most of these subsequently returned to revenue GWR stock after rebuilding from 1920 onwards.

The vehicles remained in front line service until the late 1930s, although it must be said the number of express workings on the GWR in which a uniform rake of similar style stock was used was rare, limited to few prestige workings, certainly a study of images from the period will reveal a motley selection ranging from the latest Collett stock though to the Churchward Toplight and even Clerestory vehicles in the train make up.

With time they were cascaded on to lesser duties, the longest lived vehicles and as would be expected, those destined to have the longest life being the general purpose rather than the more specialist vehicles. The final Toplight duty was either in departmental / engineering guise, or in Camping Coach mode. Here they shared work with pensioned off clerestories, although in both this form and the departmental / engineering guise, modifications and changes to suit a new role can sometime make identification difficult. The longevity of a number of Toplight coaches especially in Camping Coach role has also resulted in some 23 listed as being preserved, this compares with something in excess of 850 Toplight vehicles that were built. Just over 200 are shown as having seen military service but it is not clear if this figure is inclusive or exclusive of the total. (The figure for any vehicles possibly 'lost in action' is not known.)

The only image so far located of a Toplight coach in revenue service is that previously reproduced as part of page 26 - caption for which is on page 27. This view though is also unique in depicting a former Diagram C32 vehicle of the 'Multibar' type. Eight Third-Class compartments were provided together with a lavatory at each end. Whilst clearly either in, or perhaps redundant from what was probably departmental or possibly camping coach use, externally this vehicle has retained many original fittings although the doors appear sealed (so leading to the thought it may be a camping coach vehicle) with door and commode handles removed. Vehicles to Diagram C32 were built in 1914, 1915 and 1920, with many taken back into stock in 1921/22 after war department use. Several survive in preservation. The brackets for a roof board are perhaps a reminder of a more glorious past.

Amyas Crump

W9989W, formerly No. 2578. This is another Diagram C32 vehicle built in 1914. After an operational life of 43 years it was converted as seen in 1957, recorded at Marizion on 20 April 1961. This coach survived for a third lease of life on the West Somerset Railway. R C Riley

Inset - David Hyde

Left - A wonderful portrayal of three Toplight Camping Coach vehicles being serviced at Oswestry prior to the summer season. Nearest the camera is W9875W, formerly W3950W, an All-Third Multibar type of 1919 to Diagram C35. This vehicle was converted from capital stock in 1958 and was subsequently preserved at Llangollen. The two other coaches are both of the Diagram C31, Bars 2 type. W9923W* had been W2462W of 1913, and W9921W* formerly W2460W, built in 1913, the latter passed to the military as a WW1 'Ward Car' but returned to the Great Western and was re-converted for passenger use in December 1922. Prior to its role as a Camping Coach, it has been suggested one of these vehicles may have seen departmental service at Exeter as late as August 1983 but this is not confirmed. Neither W9923W nor W2462W survived into preservation. (Identification is made easier by the running numbers on the steps.)
* converted to Camping Coach use in 1952.

Amyas Crump

Above - An unidentified former Camping Coach, possibly a Diagram C32, at Totnes in 1968.

Colour Rail 81019

35

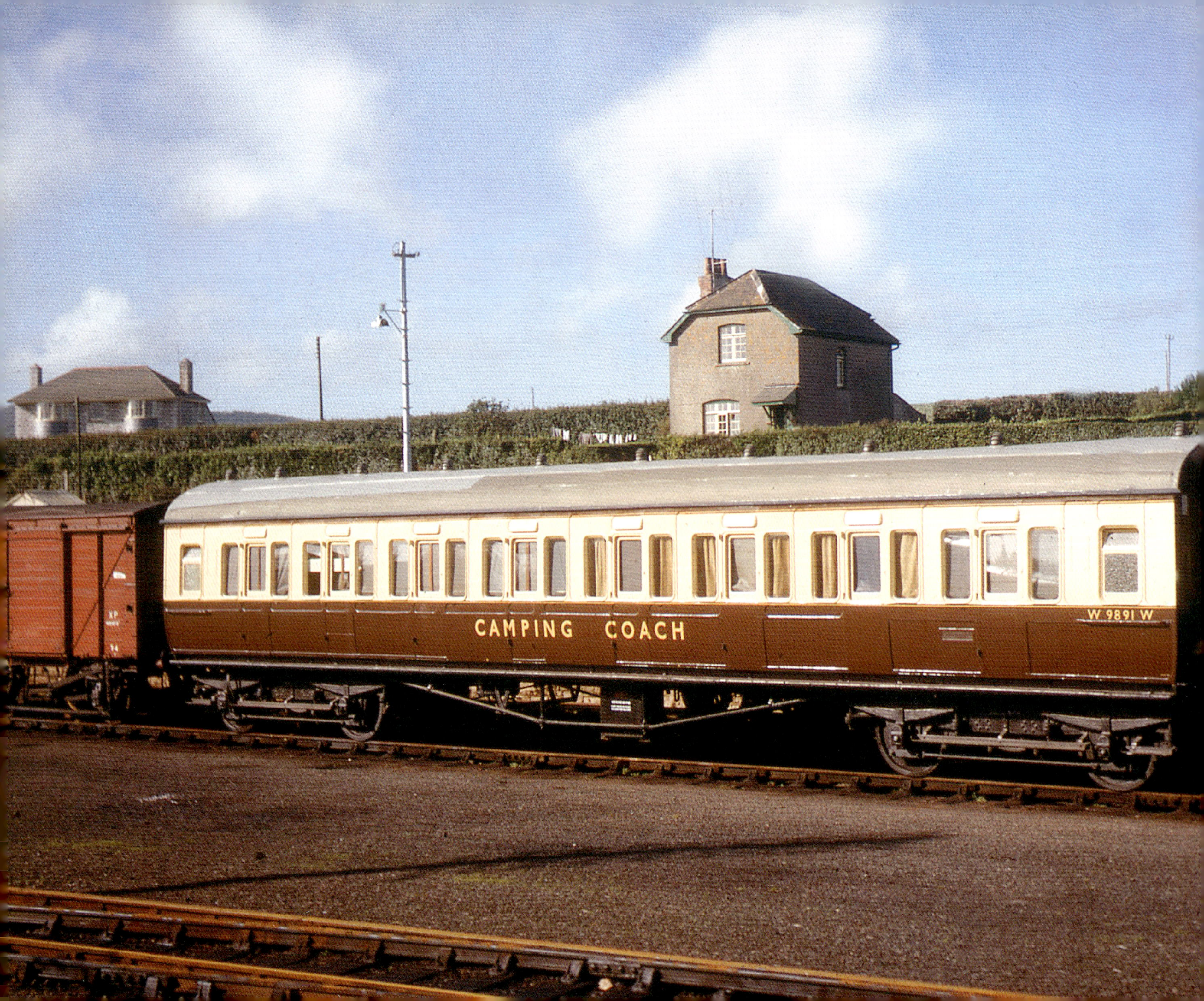
CAMPING COACH
W 9891 W

Left - W9891W clearly modified over the years both in service and for its Camping Coach role. Clearly visible is the difference in the underframe supporting trusses of this Bars 1 vehicle of 1921, compared with W9875 of the Multibar type seen on the preceding double page spread. The vehicle seen here was originally W3655W, a Diagram C28 vehicle which has seen war service as a Personnel Car in Ambulance Train No 27. It was returned to GWR service in 12/1923 to Diagram C31. This was one of 15 toplight coaches adapted for Camping Coach use in 1957.

Roy Denison

Top - Images of Toplight vehicles (other than in preservation) may be rare, but surely camping coaches on the move must be rarer still. Here the photographer has captured a train of such vehicles - identified as Toplights from the ventilator above each door, but also heavily modified over the years. The location is Aller Junction outside Newton Abbot on 14 November 1962.

Colour Rail 103310

Bottom - Captured from the adjacent main road on an unreported date, two of the three former Toplight vehicles that were located at Aberdovey. The final numbers of two of these three were W9924W and W9927W, respectively the former W2468W and W2476W, both Bars 1 type dating from 1911 and later converted for WW1 service. They returned to GWR use in late 1921, neither would survive into preservation.

Colour Rail 103316

A Diagram E.73 First / Second Composite clerestory from 1902, Lot No. 987, seen as W9906W but formerly carrying the running number (7)472. This was one of six conversions of vehicles from Diagram E.73 which took place in May 1952. During the 1950s this vehicle was based at Luxulyan (opposite), possibly even for a while in green livery, but had been repainted in conventional chocolate and cream by circa 1960. After this date, and consequent upon the withdrawal of Camping Coach facilities from certain Cornish locations, it was transferred to the Cambrian Coast at Borth (above). It was noted that heating, cooking and lighting was by paraffin. **Above -** *Jim Gander,* **Right -** *R C Riley, Luxulyan, 30 March 1960.*

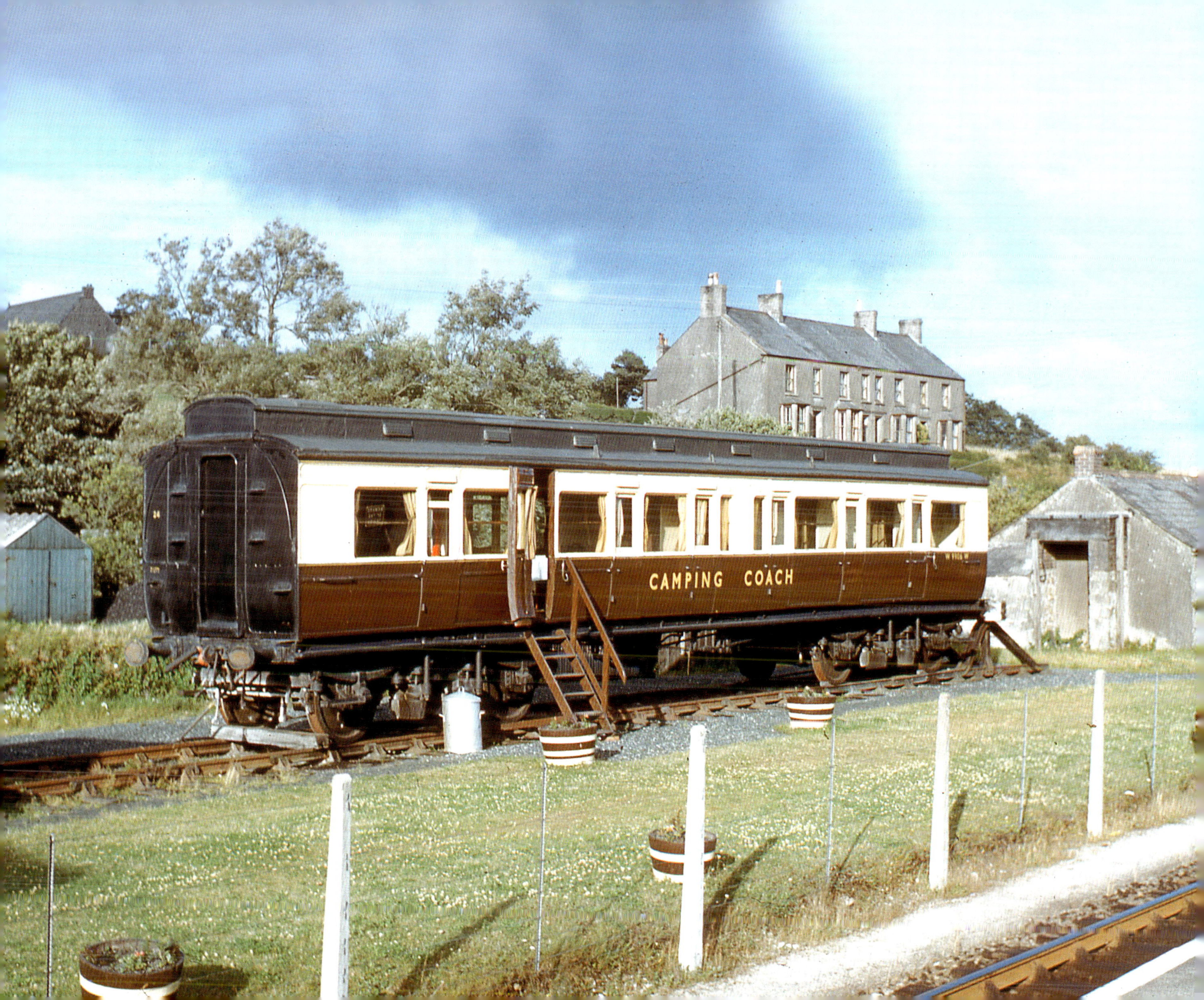
CAMPING COACH

One of the best known vehicles from GWR days and probably the last GWR vehicle to run at high speed on BR was the 'Whitewash Coach'. Built in 1911 as No. 2360, a conventional 56' Brake-Third 'Bars 1' Toplight, it was first transferred to the Experimental Section at Swindon in 1928 and fitted with 7' bogies. In this guise it performed extremely well and in consequence was selected to be a permanent Track-Testing coach to run on a regular basis behind normal service trains. Accordingly in 1932 it was stripped internally, leaving just two compartments and a lavatory intact. A tank for whitewash was installed in part of the space formerly occupied by the guard's compartment. The outlet from this tank was connected, via a system of valves, to electrical circuitry, which in turn took its own readings from vehicle bogie - not coach body - movement. At the same time a Hallade recorder was monitoring movements both lateral and vertical (four separate traces were made) as well as the locations where a 'dollop' of white had been deposited. The inset sides were for a 'spotter' to sit observing mileposts and other fixed lineside features, which would be annotated on to the trace as a precise indication as to the vehicle's location. When operational, those in the vehicle would include the Divisional Engineer or assistant, the local ganger, a spotter and a steward - who in the 1980s still served refreshments in china cups to those on board. Whilst seemingly aged externally, the internal equipment was updated on several occasions, finally including various audible warnings to indicate a possible track defect, in place of what had developed to become tanks of different coloured wash to indicate different types of track defect. (Prior to the instigation of the 'Whitewash Coach' - renumbered W139W in 1948 and later still DW139, it had been the practice to use a 68' Brake-Third from 1902, No. 2400. Testing had also taken place whereby assistants would stand at the lavatory pans of various vehicles ready to tip part of a can of whitewash down the pan every time a rough piece of track was reached.) DW139 was active until 1989, by this time also running on modern bogies but passed for 100mph. Alterations were made to the windows and panelling over the years

SPECIALIST VEHICLES

but some items remained unchanged: the compartments from 1911 still retaining their strung luggage racks and carriage prints, whilst a former GWR Ship's clock was attached to the observation end. DW139 ceased running in 1989, age plus the fact that more and more trains were now of the multiple-unit type meant that use of the test coach had to be part of a special train: locomotive - at least three empty vehicles required for brake force - and DW139. When operated in this way it was practice to run at slightly higher than the permitted speed in some places, this with the consent of the CCE. (Certain locations could be interesting - Hawkridge curve at just 5mph more than was permitted resulted in bells / claxton and warbler all coming into action at once.) The coach is now preserved by the National Railway Museum.

Opposite page - At Swindon in January 1966. Prior to 1948 livery had been chocolate and cream, post 1948 it carried crimson and cream but this had changed to that seen by 1960. The final livery was corporate blue/grey, one of a very few GWR vehicles to carry these colours. (See also page 7.) *R C Riley.*

Opposite inset - A mid 1980s glimpse recalling an earlier age. The compartment was used as a meeting place when required. BR standard blue moquette was by now used for the seat covering. *KR.*

This page - Taken prior to and during a circular 'calibration test' in the mid 1980s. This particular run was from Swindon via Melksham, Hawkridge, Heywood Road, the Berks and Hants line, Reading West Curve and Didcot. Two runs were made on the same day. The GWR clock can just be seen above the front right hand window in the lower view. *KR.*

Unlike the Whitewash coach which was a conversion from an ordinary coach, the Churchward dynamometer car was a special build. (We should perhaps more accurately refer to it as the Dean vehicle, built as it was in the last days when William Dean was in charge - albeit at the behest of his successor.) Whatever, No. 790, was officially recorded as completed on 16 March 1901 on wagon Lot No. 293 to Diagram Q20. No. 790, W7W under BR, survived in its original role for 60 years, and whilst as Michael Harris comments, "It did not share the fame of the former North Eastern car which accompanied Gresley's 'Mallard' on its record run down Stoke bank....", the Churchward vehicle contributed much to knowledge of steam working. In outline with its sloping clerestory, the vehicle was very much in contemporary Royal saloon style, but somewhat shorter at just 45' 0¾" long. As with the Whitewash coach, the internal equipment included a Hallade recorder. There was also a retractable flangeless wheel, seen in the illustrations, used for speed recordings. Other equipment is not so obvious but included cable and pipe work connections to measure drawbar pull, exhaust temperature, smokebox vacuum plus other constraints for controlled road testing. Indeed the GWR was the first British railway able to undertake scientific testing in this way. Some of its more notable outings have included 96 mph behind No. 5056 'Earl of Powis' in 1947, with various engine types during the 1948 Locomotive Exchanges, a few years later when colossal loads were being trailed behind the re-draughted members of the 'King class and shortly afterwards when similar tests were being carried out with examples of the new BR 9F class. W7W was withdrawn from service in 1961 and stored in and around the Swindon stock shed until purchased for preservation in 1965. (The accompanying images are in this location.) At this stage all of the internal equipment had been stripped, much finding a new home in the replacement Hawksworth Dynamometer Car - see page 14.

This page, top - Swindon. Jim Gander
This page, bottom - Swindon, 20 August 1964.
  Amyas Crump
Opposite page - Swindon, 16 August 1964. R C Riley

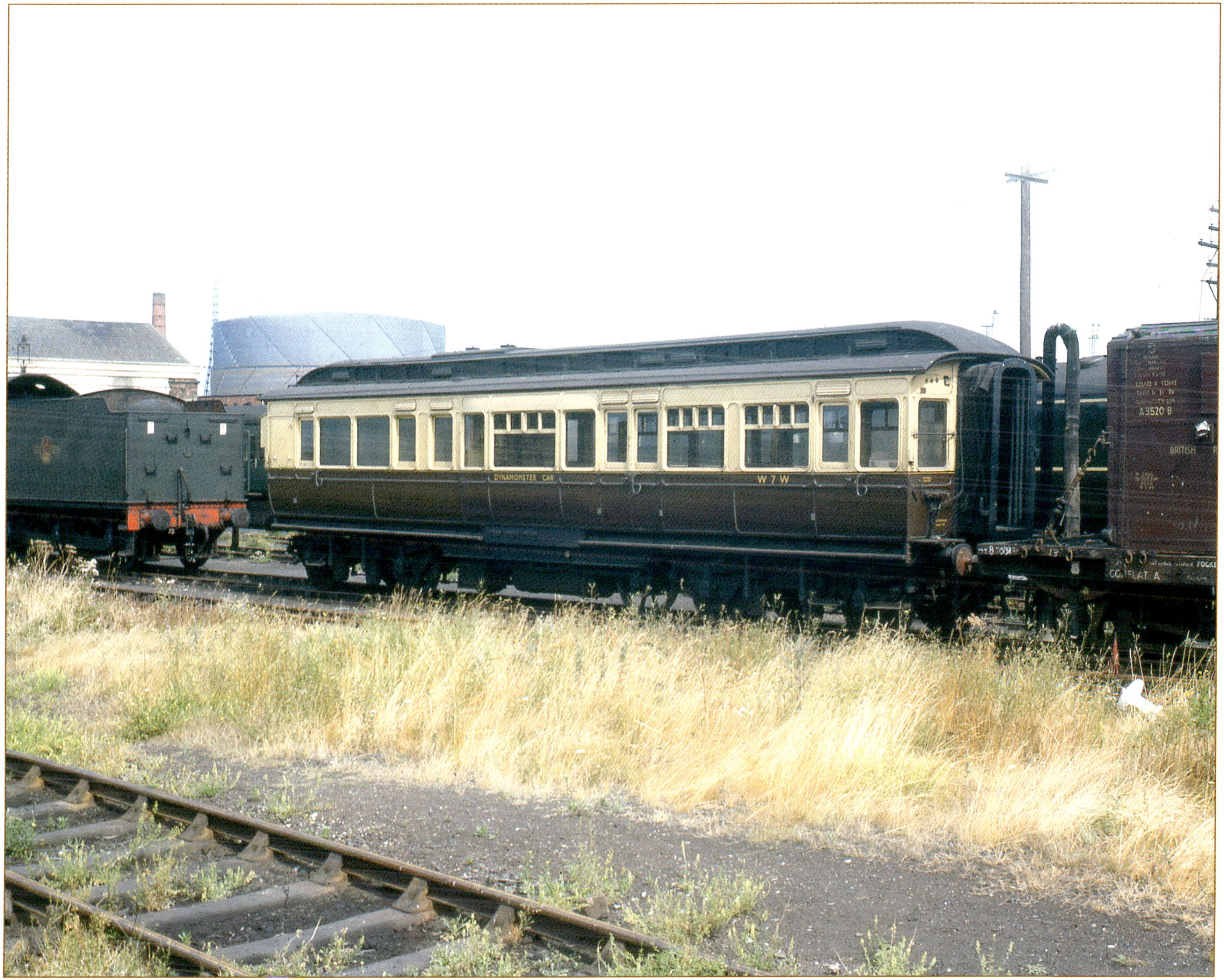
DYNAMOMETER CAR
W 7 W
A3520 B
BRITISH

RESTAURANT CARS

Dining cars were first introduced to the GWR as late as 1896, some years after the first 'Dining Room Carriage' had been introduced by the Great Northern in 1879. Indeed until 1891 it seems Paddington had been content to ignore this aspect of rail travel, but in that year a report was produced discussing the merits, and pitfalls, of introducing dining-cars. It appears a conservative GWR were unsure as to any financial benefit that might result but nevertheless three vehicles were approved and appeared in mid 1896. As befitted the style of the period, these vehicles were 56' 0¾ with a roof clerestory. Built to Lot No. 801, they were Diagram H2 (there were many gaps in the 'H' Diagram list including Diagram H1) and numbered 250-252, later renumbered 8250-3 and post 1907: 9501-3. They were originally limited to First-Class only with seating for just 16 passengers. Further vehicles to the same H2 diagram were built in in 1897 (1), and 1900 (2). All but one of these were rebuilt in the early 1900s as composite restaurant cars, the seating capacity increased to 29 achieved by the removal of the two lavatories. Two cars, Nos. 9501/2 were marshalled into Ambulance trains during WW1 to afford meals and refreshments. Consequent upon the construction of more modern catering vehicles, four of the six cars were withdrawn around 1929-31, although two, No. 9502 of 1896 and 9516 of 1900 were given a face lift and emerged as 'Café Cars' - Michael Harris refers to this as the GWR's euphemism for the latter day term of 'Buffet Car'. In this guise they had a brief reprieve but both were withdrawn in 1936 although again according to Harris, they may have seen some further use in two (unspecified) exhibition trains.

Left - A remarkable survivor. The body of the very first GWR Dining Car, the former No. 252 of 1896 (latterly No. 9501) at Liskeard in October 1961 in use as the Staff Association building. It had been withdrawn in 1931 and presumably arrived on site shortly afterwards. In service it had weighted 27 tons. An undated survey but probably from the 1950s, showed five grounded coach / van bodies at Liskeard in use for various purposes.

Bottom - Internally and discounting the obvious modern additions., much of the original panelling appears intact. It is believed this historic may still survive at a private site. Another grounded body from an early restaurant car, this time No. 9520 (as built No. 578), a 56' 0¾" H7 type of 1903 and to the same dimensions as the Liskeard body, has been saved and resides in unrestored condition at Didcot. Withdrawn and sold by the GWR in 1930, No. 9520 served as the Temperance Building at Newbury, although latterly it became a cobbler's shop.

Both - John Chamney

We may conveniently ignore the LMS coach in the foreground and concentrate initially instead on No. 9543, the magnificent 70' vehicle above. This was built to Lot 1131, Diagram H15 in 1907, one of 12 identical vehicles in the series 9534-45 and weighing 45 tons. As constructed lighting was by electricity and cooking by gas, a feature which appears to have continued unaltered - as witness the battery boxes and gas tanks attached to the underframe. There are though two main visual changes from 1907 condition, apart from the obvious livery alterations. The first of these is the coach is now running on six-wheel bogies - compared with the 4-wheel 'American' type fitted when new. According to Russell, these were added in 1938, but it is apparent also from the same source that not all the vehicles from this batch were so changed, No. 9542 for example was still running on 4-wheel bogies in 1952. The second visual alteration is the windows have been changed from the original two quarter lights and one droplight per pair of seats to the style seen. No date is given for this alteration. The view affords a good indication of how former GWR dining car stock survived in BR days for catering purposes within trains consisting otherwise of more modern BR Mk1 vehicles. By the date of the view, Old Oak Common 10 September 1960, its days were rapidly drawing to a close with only four of the original 12 remaining in service. The GWR vehicle in the train on the main line, is a Collett Third - further identification not being possible. Note however the slot to allow a coach letter board to be inserted to the left of the final window.

R C Riley

W9553W is a 70' diner from Lot 1177, Diagram H19 of 1911. Four vehicles were constructed to this Lot and in company with some similar length First-Class vehicles and Parcels vans were designated as 'Fishguard Boat Stock'. The coach is seen here at Newton Abbot on 19 July 1957 in company with a Hawksworth Brake and BR Mk1. This particular coach was reconditioned in 1936 and as well as new windows (the rounded corners were not dissimilar to the style later adopted by Bulleid) replacement 9' plate-frame bogies were fitted and side panelling applied. It is believed the other vehicles from this Lot were similarly modified around the same time, although it will be noted the retention of ventilators above the door droplights presents a somewhat dated appearance. Weighting 40 tons, this vehicle was withdrawn in 1958.

R C Riley

Just two pairs of 'Centenary' dining salons were built in 1935. Nos 9635/6 were First-Diners (Lot 1540 Diagram H43) but intended to run coupled to one of pair of Third-class diners (Lot 1541, Diagram H44, Nos. 9637/8) constructed at the same time. As turned out, they again had the large picture windows of the car type - see notes on page 21, but replacement windows of the style seen were fitted in 1938. Illustrated is No. W9636W, just outside Paddington. This First-Class car had a kitchen and pantry, the latter including a wine bin, and seats for 24 passengers in either a '2+2' or '1+ 1' setting, they were also heavy, at 42 tons. The accompanying Third-Class car could accommodate 64 passengers all in '2+2' style, but did not have any cooking facility. From a photograph in Russell taken in 1951, the sister vehicle to that seen above, No. W9635W was already separated from its dining twin by this date, possibly the original pairings not being reinstated post-war. Both first class cars and their original partners, were condemned in late 1962, W9636W having the dubious distinction of being the last GWR design catering vehicle having a regular duty from Paddington - the 6.45 pm to Weston-super-Mare. The sister vehicle to that seen, W9635W is preserved at Didcot.   Amyas Crump

Nine years after nationalisation and the sign still proclaims 'GWR (and Underground) Royal Oak Station and Ticket Office'. In recording the passing of what is probably empty stock on the way from Old Oak into Paddington, Dick Riley's photograph, taken from the Ranelagh Bridge loco servicing facility (behind the camera), reveals both a study in coach design as well as the liveries of the 1950s. Featured left, in red and cream, is what appears to be a Third-Corridor, possibly to Diagram C77. Narrowing it down even further is that it may be from Lot 1623 of 1940. The Buffet is more easily identified. This is W9677W, one of five vehicles, original running numbers 9676-80, built to Lot. 1602 in 1938 and to Diagram H55. These vehicles were fitted with 6-wheel bogies from the outset and together with the composite-diner type seen opposite and a pair of kitchen cars (not illustrated) all built around the same time, were destined to be the final 12-wheel catering vehicles constructed by the GWR. Designated as 'Buffet' cars from the outset, their introduction coincided with the trend towards snacks and light refreshments rather than a full meal. As such they were popular with management: such vehicles required less staff! Of the five vehicles, two had walnut panelling internally and three were fitted out in teak. In 1954 this particular coach was the first to be repainted in chocolate and cream and was then included in the formation of the 'Bristolian', No. W7678W was subsequently painted in like manner. By 1962 the influx of BR standard catering vehicles meant GWR coaches had been relegated to relief and excursion work. One of the five was condemned in the autumn of 1962, two others followed shortly afterwards and Nos 9676/9 were the last to go, probably in 1965. At right and in maroon, is believed to be a D104 Brake-Third corridor. The lack of a running number does not assist but it may well be from 1929.

R C Riley

Above - The final view of a public restaurant car is of No. W9672W, a 1938 12-wheel composite diner to diagram H57, Lot 1601. Five vehicles were built although they were destined to have a short initial life as many catering vehicles had been stored at locations such as Henley-on-Thames by the end of WW2. Having received little attention for some time, in 1946 No. 9672 was selected for refurbishment - the prototype for such work on all catering vehicles. The interior was attended to by Messrs Hampton & Sons - a b/w illustration of the interior of this vehicle in its refurbished form appears on page 32 of the second edition of the Michael Harris book. It re-entered service in February 1946 by which time 26 other catering vehicles has also been restored. The other vehicles from this Lot were similarly treated. After a period in red and cream livery, chocolate and cream was reapplied to Nos. 9672/3 in 1956 and the type continued on principal workings until 1960. Subsequent to this they were to be found on relief services until withdrawn in October 1962. On either side are what appear to be Diagram C64 / C65 corridor-thirds dating from 1933. Two batches of these vehicles were built one with a bow end and the other with a flat end: separate diagram numbers but unusually to the same Lot 1489. Amyas Crump

Left - Included as an example of an H57 in the make up of a train comprised otherwise solely of BR Mk1 stock. The location and date are Penzance in 1957, No. 6941 'Fillongley Hall' seen departing with the Up 'Royal Duchy'. The third vehicle (indicated) is the H57 restaurant-car, either No. 9672 or 9673.

John Chamney

SPECIAL SALOONS and INSPECTION SALOONS

In July 1940 Swindon completed the construction of two First-class saloons. Built to Lot 1626, Diagram G62, they took the numbers 9001/2, each a self contained vehicle for VIP use on daytime journeys. Carried on six-wheel bogies, these were heavy vehicles at 42 tons each. As might be expected, during WW2 they found use by senior government and military personnel (Nos. 9002 and Super Saloon 9113 were part of the train used by General Eisenhower on visits to Kingsbridge during inspection of training for D-Day in the Slapton area), radio-receiving equipment was also installed in the main saloon in 1944. As built they had a day (dining) saloon, coupé, pantry and kitchen. Accommodation was for 24 persons, although this was later reduced to 20 in consequence of extensions to the coupé and dining sections. Body length and width was as per the diagram H57 buffet cars of 1938 (illustrated on page 49), at 60' 11¼" x 8' 11". Fixed seating was provided in the dining (day) saloon but with separate arm chairs and settees in the coupé, where there were also small tables. Michael Harris describes the original interiors as 'spartan' but even so post 1945 they were allocated for Royal Train use. Notwithstanding the fact that again according to Harris they saw little use between 1945 and 1963, the interiors were re-panelled and refurbished in 1953. It is believed they carried red and cream rather than claret post 1948, but appeared again in chocolate and cream in 1960 whilst in 1963 BR decided to try and advertise them for hire to business users, it is thought only with a modicum of success. Black and white illustrations of the interior of W9001W appear in Russell Coaches Appendix Part 2. Both have been preserved, one at Tyseley and the other at Didcot.

Left - W9901W at Paddington in the early 1960s', the cleanliness of the vehicle in marked contrast to the smoke covered platform valance. The vehicle seen, plus either No. 9004/5 (see next page) and Super Saloon W9117W (see illustration page 17) were part of a Royal formation attached to an ordinary train.

Jim Gander

Top right - Sister vehicle, No. W9002 seen from the opposite side and in 'as-delivered' condition to Didcot in 1968. The roof aerial will be noted.

Amyas Crump

Bottom Right - W9001W at Paignton en-route to Kingswear. Possibly either carrying, or going to collect a dignitary in connection with the Naval College at Dartmouth, unfortunately again with the curtains drawn!

Amyas Crump

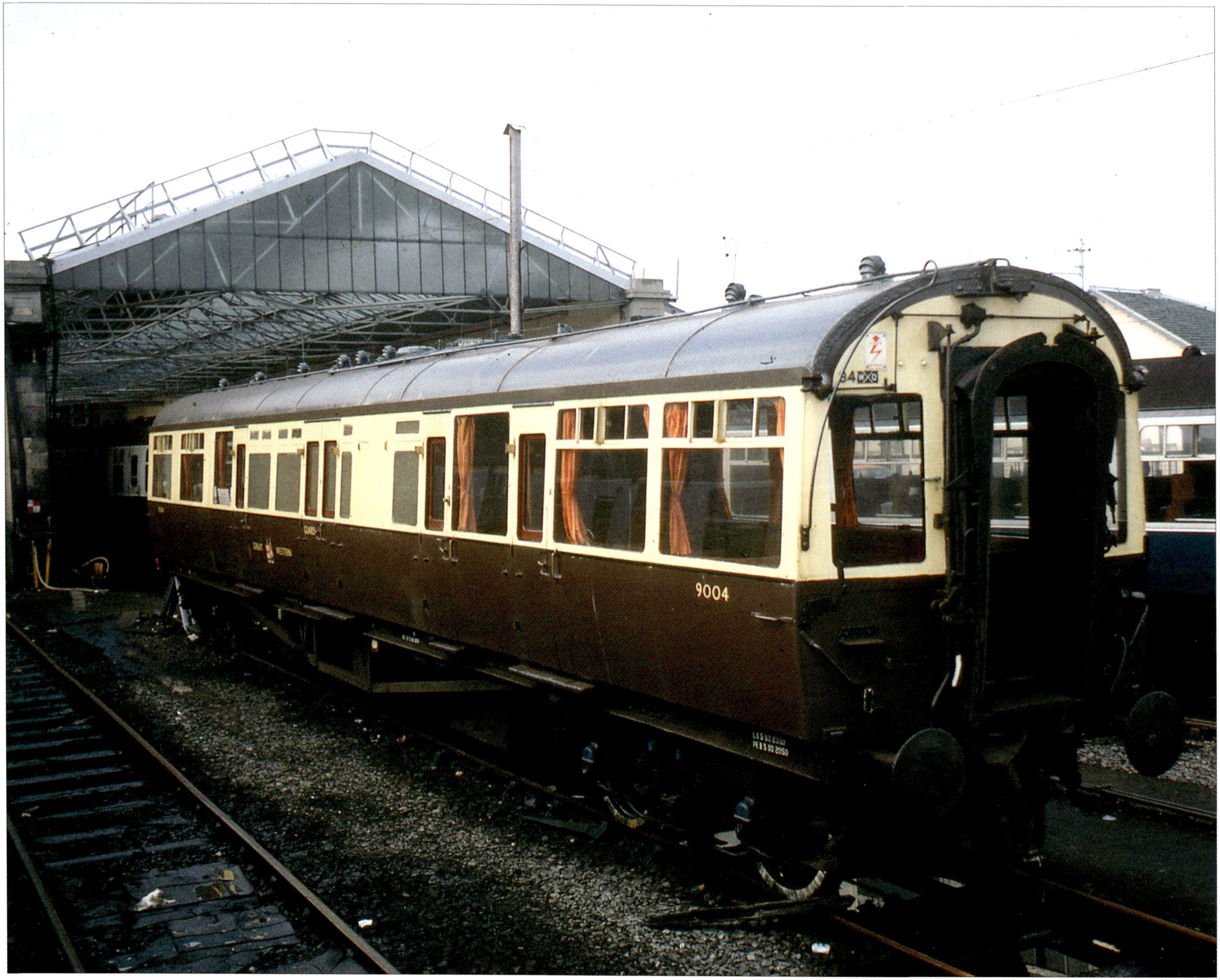
9004

In the same 'Saloon' category as 9001/2, were Nos. 9004/5 although pre-dating the earlier vehicles having been built in 1930. Intended as self-contained saloons for private hire, they could well be said to be the direct descendents of the numerous saloons available on the GWR (and other, lesser, railways) in the nineteenth century. A time when the affluent passenger might require the local station master to provide a carriage truck at short notice as well as a saloon - unless that affluence extended as far as the running of a private train! By the 1930s, saloon use had diminished greatly, so it might well be asked how much use did Nos. 9004/5 actually achieved? Clearly Paddington must have felt there was still a market for such prestige work, for whilst some of the older saloons were then still running, authority felt a more modern vehicle was needed. Whatever, the new coaches were 61' 4½" in length, and 9' wide, this width restricting their sphere of activity and coming from the bulbous sides present below the waistband. The associate curve of the sides presented a 'porky' appearance* and shows up particularly well when seen as a direct comparison with W9001W on page 51. Even so on paper there was only a one-inch difference, the curved-verses– flat(ter) side creating the visual effect. Possessing a large central kitchen, there were two separate saloons, one at either end, the view for passengers enhanced by end windows, although the necessary corridor connection presented a cluttered appearance. This piecemeal approach continued on the sides, aesthetically perhaps some of the most unattractive vehicles Swindon ever produced, but internally of course it was a different matter, sumptuous settees and loose arm chairs: there was even a radio fixed to the bulkhead. Both were altered from the original over the years including changes to the seating. They retained chocolate and cream under BR, No. 9005 undergoing the unusual transformation of a new underframe from brake-second No. 5031 in 1961. This vehicle subsequently received corporate blue/grey and was used as the WR General Manager's saloon running on modern B4 bogies - the latter developed of course at Swindon. Withdrawn in 1974 it was acquired by the Great Western Society. Sister vehicle, No. 9004, had in the meanwhile been transferred for officer use by the CCE of the North Eastern Region in 1963, it remained as such until 1972 when it was preserved by Sir William MacAlpine.

Left - *No. 9004, in BR - Great Western livery, notice the electrification flash on the end. These two vehicles were constructed to Lot No. 1431 and Diagram G59.*

Amyas Crump

Right - *No. 9004 at Olympia. The preserved NER salon is seen on the right.*
Colour Rail 81104

* Swindon coach building might well be described as appearing to go through different phases. Between 1930 and 1933 for example, a considerable number of general service stock appeared to the 9' width - even some 'B-sets' were built to a width of 9'3". This trend found its maximum in the 'Super-Saloons' and 'Centenary' with a 9' 7" width. By 1937 8' 11" was becoming more common for new construction and would become universal in later years.

53

In 1948 some long overdue replacement Engineers Inspection Saloons were constructed. Seven were built to Diagram Q13, Nos. 80943/69/70/72/74-6, the initial allocation to Newport, Neath, Shrewsbury, Wolverhampton, Bristol, Taunton and it is believed Reading. Despite the fact they were built in the first year of BR, all received chocolate and cream: W80976W, first allocated to Taunton in 1949 (subsequently TDW80976) was still carrying this, albeit by now badly faded livery, when seen at Manchester in September 1978.

Intended to run as a solitary vehicle, or at the end of a train without any risk of interference, no gangways were provided and instead they were provided with three end windows - akin to auto trailer style excepting the fact the inspection saloons had flat ends. Again like the auto trailer, they had a gong to warn of their approach when being propelled. Compared with contemporary passenger stock then being built, these were short vehicles at 52' long and 8' 11" wide, but this still allowed for a saloon at either end, with a galley, lavatory and guard's compartment in-between. Retractable steps to track level, once more like the auto-trailer design, were provided for the centre access door. Prior to 1948, and indeed for a while afterwards, a motley selection of vehicles had been used as engineers salons, most converted from former capital stock. Details of these are given on page 122 of the Michael Harris book with illustrations of several early vehicles in 'Coaches Appendix Vol. 2'.

Left - W80972W (Diagram Q13) being cleaned at Oswestry in August 1961.
Amyas Crump

Top right - The same vehicle four years later at Shrewsbury, the ravages of time having taken their toll. *Amyas Crump*

Bottom - An unidentified saloon in use at Swindon in 1965. Three of the type were withdrawn in 1972, although three others were reported as still active in 1983. W80943W (in 1948 this was the London division vehicle) had also received corporate blue/grey with a half yellow end by July 1967. All have been preserved.

55

Left - Concluding the images on Inspection Saloons is this view of the one-off DW150266, formerly an H33, 58' 4½" composite dining-car from Lot. 1549 of 1925. This was a 1960 Swindon conversion from No. 9580 and was immediately allocated to the Western Region S & T Department at Reading. It is seen in the sidings at the Signal Works on 23 November 1966. It was subsequently preserved and restored on the East Lancashire Railway.

Pat Avery

Bottom - A pair of Diagram A38 auto-trailers of 1951 vintage (see notes on this type on page 59) form the load for 64xx No. 6430 on the 12.40 pm ex Tavistock (South) to Plymouth North Road, approaching Whitchurch Down Platform, 20 December 1962.

Alastair Jeffery

THE AUTO-TRAILER BREED

Top - The solitary diagram A39 trailer of 1951. Entering service in red and cream livery as W220W it received the name 'Thrush' - sister vehicle W221W, again a 'one-off' to Diagram A40, took the name 'Wren' at the same time. The intention being to produce a 'class' of similar vehicles each carrying a bird name. Just one year after entering service, 'Thrush' was re-fitted internally with modern metal-framed seats and pastel laminate panelling - to a style that would be seen in the diesel railcars of the 1950s. Ten further vehicles to the same style as the re-equipped No. W221W were built in 1954, Diagram A43, Nos, W235W-W244W. These were also destined to be the last auto-trailers built. Neither 'Thrush' seen here at Dulverton with an Exe Valley train, nor 'Wren' would survive, although two vehicles from the 1954, Diagram A43 built have reached preservation.

Great Western Society

Bottom - An unknown example of the final Diagram A43 type at Churston with the Brixham branch train, 6 October 1954. The red colouring for the coach in this view creates a vivid comparison with that seen above and whilst the temptation is to blame the film or computer 'colour manipulation' - the latter has not been undertaken, attention should be drawn to the arms of the signals seen in the two views. These are without doubt to the standard 'signal-red' colour which consequently begs the question what shade of red was being used for the respective coaches?

Colour Rail 102989

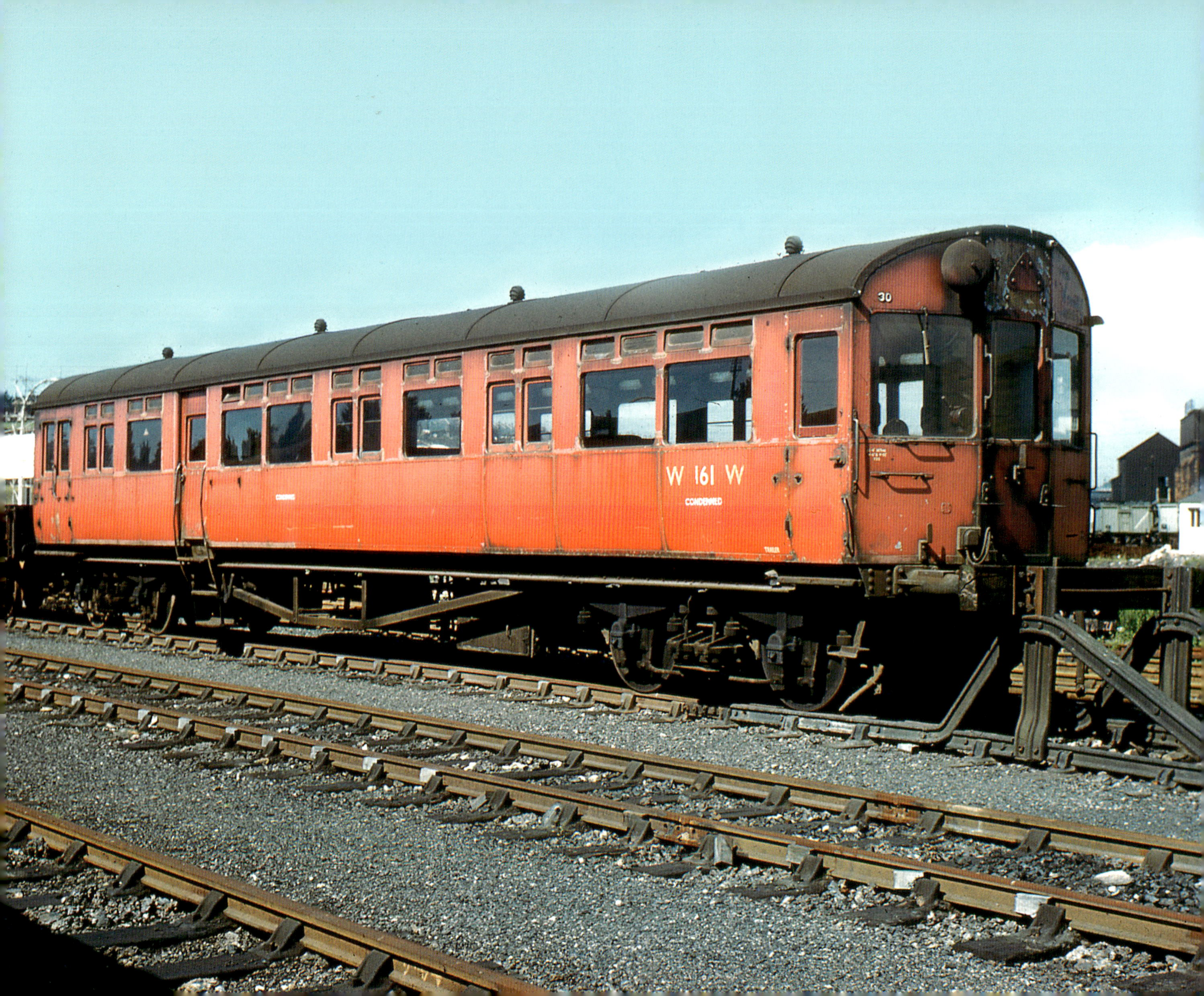

W 161 W
CONDEMNED
30

*Twenty-two years separate the building of the auto-trailers seen on these pages, that on the **left** W161W, to Lot 1394 (Diagram A27) of 1929. Twelve were constructed, Nos. 159-170, 59' 6" long and 9' wide. They could accommodate 72 passengers. Of interest was that in keeping with all other early trailers, these vehicles had end windows - perhaps more accurately referred to as 'end lights' at the luggage end of the vehicle. From Diagram A38 onwards, the ends were either plain or plated over. W161W is seen at the end of its life, at Laira, 17 July 1961, having only recently been taken out of traffic. Although clearly no longer in service, it is interesting that the designation 'Condemned' has been painted on in stencil - even at the end of its life certain standards still applied! The **above** scene is at Tiverton on 15 June 1962. 14xx No. 1434 heads north with two vehicles, that nearest the camera W228W, a 1951 built vehicle to Diagram A38, Lot No. 1736. Thirteen vehicles were built to this diagram, Nos. 222-34, two others, Nos. 220 and 221, constructed to the same Lot number, but both different internally from each other as well as being different from the main batch. Diagram A38 vehicles were some of the last in service, their lives cut short by dieselisation and branch closures. Despite the difference in ages between the two vehicles seen, the basic layout of the auto-coach design remained the same, the principal visual difference being the window design. The A38 vehicles were slightly longer at 64', but one inch narrower than their older counterpart, however they only had 68 seats so could accommodate fewer passengers. Four A38 diagram vehicles have been saved, W228W now resident at Buckfastleigh (W228 had formed part of the last passenger train from Tiverton). Having been built by BR, the A38 type received red and cream from new. W161W was destined to be scrapped, but three others from the same batch did reach preservation.*   *Both: R C Riley*

Top left - As with W161W seen previously, two views of auto-trailers at the end of their lives and both destined for the scrap merchant. Top is W29W at the unlikely location of Highbridge on 2 June 1962. This was a purpose built 70' trailer dating from January 1906, Lot 1108, of Diagram 'L'. These cars were originally provided with end windows to the luggage ends, however, they were painted over in black in 1935 and plated over sometime after. Four separate Lots of these vehicles were built, a total of 30 vehicles. All were condemned in the 1950s. Three, including W29W found further use in departmental service: the vehicle illustrated was officially withdrawn in April 1955 and as seen had clearly been abandoned for some time. It was still extant at least two months after the photograph was taken. As might be expected various bogie and other changes took place to the different types of auto-trailer over the years and these are detailed in the excellent John Lewis books - see bibliography.
Roy Denison

Bottom left - Another 70' trailer, this time to Diagram 'P' dating from May 1907. W49W was one of four identical vehicles built to Lot. No. 1130. Externally they were identical to the Diagram 'L' vehicles, the difference between the two being the seating. This vehicle had a particularly long life, not being condemned until February 1960. Its final time spent 'on loan' to the Motive Power Department at Old Oak Common, it is recorded here, possibly at Shepherds Bush.
Great Western Society

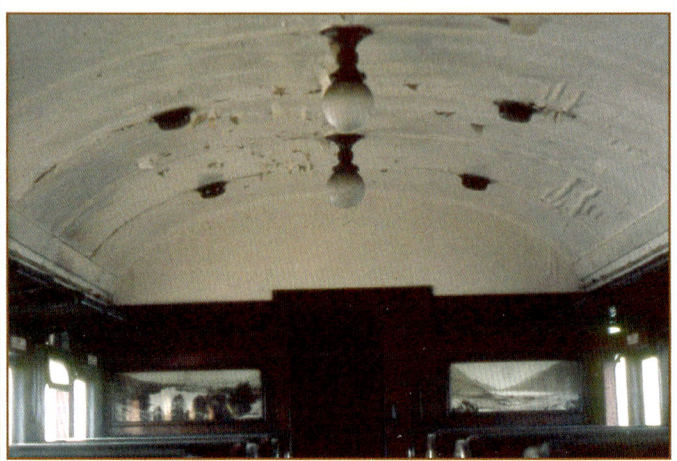

Above - An example of gas-lighting in an unrecorded Great Western vehicle. *Amyas Crump*

Right - W174W is a 1930 built steel panelled 62' 8" trailer, Lot 1410, Diagram A28. It was still extant in chocolate and cream in July 1951 but at this stage may well have gone straight into red / maroon so missing out red and cream completely. Together with it is believed the identical No. W176W, some of its last work was on the Cholsey to Wallingford branch. This particular vehicle was condemned in August 1961 but reinstated into departmental use as DW150313 in January 1962 for the use of the WR Traffic Manager. It was recorded here condemned at Oswestry on an unreported date but was destined to survive in preservation on the Swindon & Cricklade railway.

Amyas Crump

Left - A unique survivor from a bygone age although not an auto-trailer. This is W263W, one of two former Barry Railway brake coaches (the other was W268W), converted to gas-lighting at Swindon, and transferred to the Culm Valley branch in 1950. (They replaced Dean Clerestory Brake-Thirds to Diagram D37 on the branch.) They were built in 1920, were 54' 6" long, 8' 9" wide and weighed 26 tons. Their longevity was due to the slow speed of branch trains being considered insufficient to provide enough charge for an axle driven dynamo. Consequently they were also destined to be the very last gas-lit vehicles operating on British Railways. The view was taken at Uffculme on 7 August 1961.

Roy Denison

RELICS FROM AN EARLIER AGE

Left - Snapped from a passing train at Cholsey on 7 August 1965 was this view of a 4-wheel brake in engineer's service. From the limited amount of information that may be gleaned from the image, it would appear to be a Diagram T36, 4-wheel brake-third, Lot 978 of 1901. This year was clearly getting close to the end of the 4-wheel coach era as Swindon finally ceased building 4-wheel coaches at the end of 1902. Ten T36 coaches were built, Nos. 942 and 949-57 with two subsequently converted for camping coach use in 1936. One at least was subsequently used in WW2 by both the Engineering and then later the S & T departments, this being No. 9946, as built No. 951. It must be possible that this is that survivor, which had seen WW2 service at Barry, Fladbury and then with the S & T at Reading. Despite its longevity it was subsequently scrapped.

Colour Rail 103007

Left - A remarkably clean No. 4969 'Shrugborough Hall' leaving St Annes Park with an Up local (running-in turn) in 1956. Apart of course from the clean locomotive and Collett passenger stock, the principal item of interest is the first vehicle, now No. 1069, one of pair of former Royal Brake vans from the 1887 Royal Train. These were 56' 0¾" vehicles having a corridor connection at only one end. They were converted to stores vans for the company Hotels and Restaurant Department in 11/1932 and given the numbers 1069/70. Different diagrams numbers were allocated, respectively K12 and K13. .

Colour Rail BRW355 / P M Alexander

62

Top - No album of colour images of Great Western stock would be complete without a view of a 'Dreadnought'. This is the sole surviving example of the type, built in 1905, it is a nine-compartment Third to Lot. No. 1098, Diagram C.24. Fourteen were built to this particular Lot, with other types: Restaurant, Composite-Diner, Brake-Third etc also constructed. In many respects these monster vehicles, 70' x 9.6" - hence the provision of the recessed doors, were ahead of their time. Michael Harris affords an excellent summary of their pros and cons which need not be repeated here. Suffice to say they were not universally welcome by a conservative public although others, perhaps more forward looking, could see the advantage. Most had been demoted from front-line service by the early 1950s and it was indeed fortunate that No. 3299 was rescued by the Great Western Society in 1964. (Its longevity down to the fact it had survived for some time at Newquay as a hostel for restaurant car staff working up on early summer Saturday trains. It was preserved initially at Totnes but later moved to Didcot and is currently the subject of long term restoration. *Amyas Crump*

Bottom - A relic from another age. A grounded body at Felin Fach in 1965. Expert opinion is divided on its origins and in consequence both options are given. The first choice is a former 4-wheel Family Saloon from 1884, Lot 304, later Diagram G42. Originally numbered 503-7 this was changed in 1907 to 9061-5. Altered to Fruit and Parcels Vans in 1928 to Diagram O28 and renumbered 1316/7, 1319-21. The second option is a 6-wheel Family Saloon from the same year, Lot 305, Diagram G34, Nos 508-11, post 1907 Nos. 9066-9. Altered for the same purpose in 1928, to Diagram O29 and renumbered 1324-6, & 1329. The bodies of both were identical but clearly the running gear was different. No doubt also now gutted internally, this was a last lease of operational life as all were withdrawn in 1932-35. There is no confirmation when the bodywork alterations seen were carried out - possibly when it became a store. *Austin Attewell*

Another 4-wheel survivor in the mid 1960s and in the more usual engineer's black was No. W9937W, a 3-centre (refers to the roof shape) Brake-Third to Lot No. T38, Diagram T34 of 1895, originally No. 2657. It was condemned in 1938 but reinstated and converted for camping coach use the following year. Three of these saw departmental service in WW2, W9937W recorded as with the S & T department at Yeovil Pen Mill in September 1942. Other vehicles from this diagram were still in service in miners' trains during the 1950s. This coach was finally condemned in November 1965. Also at Oswestry on the same date was a former Brake 3rd of 'South Wales' stock.

Amyas Crump